21 Money Habits That Can Stabilize Your Business and Keep You Sane

A GUIDEBOOK

Nancy Rae Evans

Embracing Money Publications
KNOXVILLE, TENNESSEE

Copyright © 2015 by Nancy Rae Evans. All rights reserved. No part of this publication may be reproduced, distributed or transmitted in any form or by any means, including photocopying, recording, or other electronic or mechanical methods, without the prior written permission of the publisher, except in the case of brief quotations embodied in critical reviews and certain other noncommercial uses permitted by copyright law. For permission requests, contact permissions@embracingmoney.com.

Disclaimer: The purpose of this book is to educate and entertain. The author and publisher do not guarantee that anyone following these techniques, suggestions, tips, ideas, or strategies will become successful. They shall have neither liability nor responsibility to anyone with respect to any loss or damage caused, or alleged to be caused, directly or indirectly, by the information contained in this book.

Please visit our website: **www.Embracing Money.com**

Copy editing: Stephanie Gunning, Lincoln Square Books LLC
Book Layout ©2013 BookDesignTemplates.com

Ordering Information: Special discounts are available on quantity purchases by corporations, associations, and others. For details, contact orders@embracingmoney.com.

21 Money Habits That Can Stabilize Your Business and Keep You Sane/ Nancy Rae Evans. —1st ed.

ISBN 978-0-9963501-0-5 (paperback)
ISBN 978-0-9963501-1-2 (ebook)

Library of Congress Control Number: 2015906554

To Sunny

I dedicate this book to Sunny, an unexpected gift from the Universe. Her big brown eyes, short little legs, and gigantic attitude bring joy to my heart and laughter to my days!

The only thing that interferes with my learning is my education.

—ALBERT EINSTEIN

TABLE OF CONTENTS

Introduction		*1*
Habit 1	Make Your Sanity a Priority	3
Habit 2	Take Small Sips, Instead of Gulps	7
Habit 3	Swap Out Some Savings	9
Habit 4	Expect the Unexpected	13
Habit 5	Go Cold Turkey on Credit	17
Habit 6	Shift Some Liabilities	19
Habit 7	Don't Spend Income Before You Receive It	23
Habit 8	Ask Yourself Good Questions	25
Habit 9	Know Where Your Money Goes	27
Habit 10	Supervise Your Bookkeeper's Decisions	31
Habit 11	Regularly Give Yourself Time Off	33
Habit 12	Share the Wealth with Yourself	35
Habit 13	Know How Much Is Really Coming In	39

Habit 14	Base This Month's Spending on Last Month's Income	41
Habit 15	Achieve Your Dreams by Creating a Business Spending Plan	45
Habit 16	Resist the Urge to Pay Off Debt Quickly	49
Habit 17	Seek Out Sexy Substitutions	51
Habit 18	Hit the Pause Button	53
Habit 19	Downsize Spending While Your Business Ramps Up	55
Habit 20	Connect with Your Credit Cards	57
Habit 21	Keep It Clean with Uncle Sam	59
Acknowledgments		*61*
Resources		*63*
About the Author		*65*

INTRODUCTION

I am going to share a dirty little secret about running your own business. There's something that happens to all of us that no one wants to talk about. This secret is the main reason I decided to write this book. I wanted to shed light on it so that you won't have to suffer in silence, feeling like you're the only one facing this problem, when it happens to you.

Your income is going to fluctuate. Sometimes you'll be flooded with cash. Other times you'll have only a meager trickle of cash coming in.

It's a fact.

The sooner you accept the fact that you'll have dry seasons now and then, and implement a plan for dealing with these times of reduced income, the better off you will be.

This book reveals twenty-one habits that you can use to improve your cash flow, the life-blood of any business. With flow come financial stability and a sense of control. Feeling in control is what will help you maintain your sanity.

I've done my best to give you a balanced blend of tips for saving, tips for earning, and tips for reducing expenses. Put these together and you'll have a very simple strategy that can begin to change the financial picture of your business instantly, leading little by little, increment by increment, to a permanent and significant transformation.

The money habits are straightforward and proven effective in real life by real businesswomen. Every tip I've included comes right out of the work I do as a money coach with my clients. In my vision of an ideal world, you will begin implementing these suggestions one or two per week over the next ninety days. It won't be long before you will be noticing incredible progress from where you stand today.

Take my advice and you'll be glad you did because you won't have to suffer from cash flow fluctuations in darkness and silence anymore. You'll have inoculated yourself against inevitable shortfalls.

Let the light shine into your world!

To your success,

Nancy

Nancy Rae Evans
EmbracingMoney.com

HABIT 1

MAKE YOUR SANITY A PRIORITY

Every coaching business has upturns and downturns. Influxes of new clients—like you'd see during a program launch—bring income in. Times when clients go missing or don't re-enroll as expected can set us back.

Smooth out the impact of your fluctuating income levels by moving a small amount of income into a Sanity Fund on a regular basis. This is essentially a savings account where you'll hold cash in reserve just in case you have a bill to pay when you're facing an income shortage.

Your Sanity Fund is intended as a safety net for you and your business.

Invest in a "Sanity Fund"

Since your business likely has many moving parts—including dozens, if not hundreds, of financial transactions each month—doing business is a balancing act of money coming in and money going out.

You have income from your one-on-one VIP clients, group coaching programs, automated home-study programs, and gift certificate options. Along with selling and delivering each of these products or services come sales expenses and overhead: marketing and advertising costs, commissions due to joint venture partners, rent or a mortgage for office space, technology, virtual assistants, and other team members. Let's not forget your investment in your own training to keep growing and stretching as a businessperson yourself.

By putting money into your Sanity Fund weekly—or even daily, if you want to—it will be easier for you to build up the balance of your cash reserves than it would be if you waited and tried to fund this account once a month, or even twice a month.

Remember, the number one challenge of all businesses is having sufficient cash flow. If you don't have a positive cash flow, you won't stay in business very long. Without cash to spare, you might not be able to take advantage of great opportunities that must be acted upon immediately.

Bottom line: The more breathing room you have in your cash flow, the more ease you'll experience in your business.

A Painless Plan

Here's how to plan for the inevitable fluctuations in your income in a relatively painless way.

Every week, transfer 5–10 percent of your income from that week into your Sanity Fund. If you happen to get a big (for you) "payday" that week, I would suggest 10 percent. If your income is modest a particular week, then 5 percent is fine.

Keep investing until you reach your target goal. I suggest starting with a target of $3,000. Increase your goal until you have a full average month's income in your Sanity Fund.

If you receive income every day, perhaps due to online sales, then you may want to save some of your income on a daily basis.

This is how you create a Sanity Fund for your business.

When you hit a slow month or period, you can withdraw an amount from this savings account that enables you to meet your monthly expenses for your business and/or life. That's what it's there for! Replace the funds you borrow from the account the same way you built them up: one day or one paycheck at a time.

❧

A good part of what I do with my private clients is to help them create a monthly financial plan. If you're working with a plan like this, include your Sanity Fund as a fixed expense—a fixed percentage when you're creating your monthly plan at the beginning of the month. That way saving for your sanity rapidly becomes a meaningful money habit that helps you stay balanced financially and emotionally even when you experience a hiccup in your sales cycles.

※

HABIT 2

TAKE SMALL SIPS, INSTEAD OF GULPS

Many people who make monthly savings goals don't adhere to their savings plans because they're not in the habit of saving. Saving has to be done on a regular basis for it to become engrained.

The secret of making your new savings habit stick is to do it in small enough chunks that it doesn't restrict your cash flow. It's like taking sips instead of gulps of water.

This is why I recommend that you focus on a percentage rather than a specific dollar amount. Because as your business grows, so will your savings—automatically!

What you'll notice—especially if saving money is new to you—is that once you have the experience of saving it becomes easier and more fun. Challenge yourself to increase the amount a little at a time as you delight in watching your money reserves grow, perhaps for the first time!

To begin, choose an amount that feels easy and painless. What's important is not the amount that you're putting aside, but that the habit is being strengthened. You will feel the "pain" less if you divide your total goal into two monthly installments—or even four. This way it won't feel as threatening to your financial stability, right? Move the money weekly and you'll barely notice its absence.

HABIT 3

SWAP OUT SOME SAVINGS

If you have little or no money in your Sanity Fund right now, then it's time to make a focused effort to create this foundation of savings to stabilize your cash flow and preserve your sanity.

The goal? To "find" $1,500–2,500 as quickly as possible for your Sanity Fund.

You need to give this account a boost to put you on a solid footing.

"Where will this money come from?" you ask. *(Yes, I heard you asking that question.)*

Since stabilizing your business and preserving your sanity are both about managing cash flow, part of the money you need can be materialized simply by changing your spending habits. Whatever you choose to do to free up some cash, move that money into your Sanity Fund.

An obvious tweak that will enable you to redirect your income and quickly grow your Sanity Fund is simply shaving your spending for a couple of months.

Relax! Don't panic. I'm not advocating you go without—or depriving yourself—just doing things a little differently for a few months.

Swap a New Activity for an Old One

Do you really need to buy that new dress or those new sunglasses *this month?* Would a month or two without purchasing a new item of clothing (or insert your favorite indulgence) kill you? Maybe you and your girlfriends could "shop" in one another's closets instead.

Can you explore some lower-cost restaurants for a while, maybe finding a BYOB place where you can save a bundle by bringing your own wine or beer with you? Or... could you give yourself a break from alcohol for a month?

How about inviting the neighbors over for an old-fashioned potluck or pizza night, instead of taking the kids out? This is a great bonding opportunity for parents and kids alike.

One of my clients attends a regular crafting night with her girlfriends. Instead of going out to a noisy bar, they meet at someone's apartment and bring their projects, snacks, and a beverage of choice. Now they enjoy hanging out and expressing themselves through creative outlets—and they're saving a ton of money in the process!

Instead of an expensive lunch with a referral partner, what if you took a walk in the park or met in an art gallery? Who says business must center on food?

Who knows? You might even discover that you enjoy your new, more affordable choices more than your old more expensive ones.

※

Many types of professionals split hours in an office or wellness center. If you've got a space you're already paying for, renting it out for certain hours or days can be a way to cut your overhead expenses, making it easier to save.

If you're starting out, you could find someone with a compatible business and share space with them instead of having your own exclusive office. It's fairly common to see a nutritionist sharing with an acupuncturist or a massage therapist sharing with a chiropractor. This strategy is also a great way to get referrals!

When you're ready to grow into a second location, sharing an office with someone else in another town or neighborhood might be a great way to bring your business to a whole new market. In fact, this could be a very sophisticated strategy of you found two or three partners who were willing to rotate as a kind of consortium.

HABIT 4

EXPECT THE UNEXPECTED

If you could implement only ONE of the money habits in this book, this is the one I would most want you to embrace.

You've got to expect the unexpected.

You drop your cell phone in the toilet. Your computer catches a virus that results in a big tech-geek invoice or the need to purchase a new device. You get a flat tire on the way to an important meeting. A new client postpones his or her start date. Revisions need to be made on your website. You decide you just can't wait another year before signing up for that next training program you need.

You get the picture, right?

An important category of unexpected expenses is simply composed of those that don't happen every month.

Some of these types of expenses could be anticipated, but because they don't show up every month they tend to sneak up on us. In this case, we're talking about car repairs, annual premiums or organizational dues, insurance deductibles, the cost of summer camp for your kids, and so on.

In my opinion, "unexpected" expenses are the kinds of expenses that lead to debt and unstable finances—when you lack a plan and resources for dealing with them.

Occasional expenses that you haven't planned for can severely constrict your cash flow, the life blood of any business or household, or cause you to pull out your credit card and increase your debt. The best method I know for coping with them is to spread the pain across the entire calendar year. The approach is similar to depositing small amounts of cash weekly in one of the Christmas Club savings plans that used to be popular at banks and credit unions years ago, except that the purpose of this account is ongoing.

Use the Past to Predict the Future

What if there was a way to predict the unpredictable without having a crystal ball? There is!

1. Gather up the last twelve months of your old bank and credit card statements.

2. Highlight all the non-monthly expenses that you find.

3. Then add them up.

4. Add an extra $1,000–$2,000 to the total you got, to build in a cushion. This will become your savings goal for a second savings account: your Crystal Ball Account.

To determine how much money you'll need to contribute to your Crystal Ball Account on a monthly basis, divide your overall figure for the year by twelve. Begin contributing that amount each month. What you're doing is spreading these expenses evenly across the calendar year.

When trying to predict their non-monthly spending needs, some people find it useful to go through their previous year's calendars as well as their old financial statements to help jog their memories—particularly about once a year expenses that they can expect to happen again in the current year or at sporadic intervals.

Use this savings habit for both your personal and business finances, and in a relatively few months you will finally feel in control of your money.

No more unpleasant financial surprises!

If you are a homeowner, you'll observe that this plan works just like the escrow fund for your mortgage payment, which is set up to enable you to pay for real estate taxes and your homeowners insurance. Money goes in each month that you make your payment, and the premiums and taxes are paid in full when they come due.

HABIT 5

GO COLD TURKEY ON CREDIT

Before you panic, I'm not suggesting you stop using your credit cards completely. Rather, as an easy way for you to spend less so you can grow your Sanity Fund or Crystal Ball Account, declare a credit-free week once a month.

Studies show that we spend anywhere from 20–30 percent more if we use credit cards. That's because we don't feel the immediate impact of our purchases as much as we do when we pay cash or use a debit card.

This means that the average person (though of course, *you* are closer to *brilliant* than average if you're reading this book) will spend 20–30 percent *less* during the weeks you refrain from charging on a credit card, which potentially results in more money in your pocket that can be moved into your savings.

Carry cash during credit-free weeks and you'll get the most psychological benefit from the prohibition on plastic.

Stretch a Little to Save More

During your credit-free week, see if you can stretch yourself to move 20 percent (instead of the usual 5–10 percent) of your income into your Sanity Fund. If you can't yet, that's okay. The biggest objective is to halt unconscious, habitual spending.

This habit will become easier and easier as you repeat it each month, as you'll find that your overall spending goes down simply because you're making more conscious decisions.

Apply this habit every other week and you'll see twice the impact!

HABIT 6

SHIFT SOME LIABILITIES

Since stabilizing your business and preserving your sanity are both about managing cash flow, you should get in the habit of thinking outside of the box when it comes to managing your debt and other expenses. Consider shifting some of your existing liabilities.

"What the heck is she talking about?" (Yes, I heard you.) If you are carrying a balance on your credit cards yet you usually pay more than the minimum amount each month, you could "find" a chunk of money very quickly simply by reducing the amount you pay.

For a month or two (or three, four, five, or more), reduce your credit card payments to just the bare minimums and make a habit of redirecting an amount equal to the extra dollars you were paying into your Crystal Ball Account instead.

This small tweak with the bills you're already paying can help you to increase your savings quickly and make your life and business more sustainable over the long run.

Something Else You Could Do...

As long as you're already making your credit card and car payments on time, every time, the following suggestion is a wonderful way to give a boost to your savings once or twice a year depending on the regulations on your accounts.

Try requesting that a payment due date on one of your credit cards be moved out by two to three weeks. This will give you an extra two to three weeks of income before your next payment comes due.

In some cases, to get the date changed you simply have to phone the company and make the request. In other cases, it can be done with a few clicks online. It's rare for them to refuse.

Many credit card companies allow you to do this every six months or so. Your car loan may allow it automatically the first time you request it and require you to ask for permission for future times.

This habit can be especially helpful if you always pay your balance in full every time your bill comes. Even if you don't pay your balance in full, you can still benefit.

First things first. Ensure that you've allocated the usual amount of money for your next payment so it's there, in your checking account, when you need it on the new due date.

Now, take a portion of the "extra" income that comes in before the new due date (as much as 15–30 percent) and move that amount into your chosen savings account.

Remember that the point of the whole exercise is to increase savings. You are making a conscious choice to redirect the money you free up into your newly established Sanity Fund or Crystal Ball Account.

Caution: This extra two-week to three-week window of having cash on hand prior to making your card payment is NOT an excuse to go out and increase your spending.

HABIT 7

DON'T SPEND INCOME BEFORE YOU RECEIVE IT

It's time to stand on my soapbox for a moment.

Many business coaches these days teach people how to sell a package of several sessions instead of a single session. I love the concept . . . for the most part. Investing in a package of sessions can keep your clients moving forward with you long enough that they can begin to get better, more consistent results. It also keeps them engaged with you.

What I don't love—and in fact, this is why I realized I needed to become a more visible presence in the coaching and holistic business world—is that these coaches tend to teach you to count *promised* sales as income. They're not! At least, not immediately.

Promised sales are just that—a promise. Putting someone on a payment plan means that money *could* be coming your way. And probably is coming your way. But maybe it's not.

Have you ever had a potential client say yes and then disappear after their first payment? Or halfway through receiving the package you sold them, they claim they don't see enough benefit and want their money back?

The moral of the story: Only count money as REAL money when it lands in your bank account. Until money actually shows up "live" and "in person," it might as well be play money, like you would use in a board game.

In short, think of promised future payments as play money until they actually come in. You can dream about what you may do with this income, even make a list of ideas for how to spend it so that you don't forget them. Just don't make purchases or commitments on a credit card, thinking that you'll have the money by the time your bill is due.

You don't—at least not just yet.

Spending play money is a really great way to put yourself in debt and jeopardize the stability of your business.

In our materialistic world, it's easy to fall into believing that owning something we don't currently have will make us happier, better, sexier, and so on. In reality, the glow of a new purchase usually only lasts a few days, while the payments may go on for years (such as in the case of a car).

When faced with a big spending decision, it can be helpful to institute a seventy-two-hour grace period between decision and purchase. This gives you time to integrate your values with your decision. You may sometimes find that giving yourself permission to buy what you want is satisfaction enough, and on second glance you'll choose to put your resources elsewhere.

HABIT 8

ASK YOURSELF GOOD QUESTIONS

The human brain is an amazing instrument. It never fails to give us answers to the questions we ask of it, which is why it's so important to ask ourselves good questions.

When it comes to your business and healthy cash flow, the same question must be asked—and answered—four times before you spend any money.

Take a deep breath and listen for the answer within you each time you ask. Each time you ask the question put the emphasis on a different word.

- Do **I** really need this? (Emphasis on I)
- Do I **really** need this? (Emphasis on REALLY)
- Do I really **need** this? (Emphasis on NEED)
- Do I really need **this**? (Emphasis on THIS)

By making the above Q&A a habit for any purchasing decision you're facing, you'll automatically make more conscious choices that are aligned with your true needs.

You can also use this habit in your personal life. For example, you could rely on this habit to spend less when you're ordering meals in restaurants. Steak or salad? Wine or water? Healthier choices often cost less, so this habit may be good for your health as well as your wealth.

※

Emotional spending can be interrupted by slowing down long enough to inquire about needs. What is a need? Psychologist Abraham Maslow defined a hierarchy of needs: basic needs, psychological needs, and self-fulfillment needs. Basic needs include physical and safety/security needs. Psychological needs include love, belonging, and esteem needs.

※

HABIT 9

KNOW WHERE YOUR MONEY GOES

If you're used to ignoring the details of your finances (perhaps because it makes you anxious), then the benefit of this habit may seem counterintuitive. Nonetheless...

Knowing EXACTLY what's going on financially will help you to relax and stop stressing about money. That's right. LESS stress means more sanity. It's the avoidance of your situation that actually causes your stress, because there is a part of you that is always on high alert trying to figure out if you're going to be okay. It's like trying to sleep with one eye open.

Before you can get anywhere financially, you need to identify your starting location. Then you can get to any destination you desire.

Knowing where you money goes is similar to using a GPS. Have you ever noticed that a GPS gives you useless information while you're in a parking lot? It's like you're in a dead zone. It's only after you get out of the parking lot and onto the road that the GPS begins to provide good directions.

Until you know where your money is going, you're stuck in the parking lot.

Here's What You Can Do

Buy a small notebook to record your spending. Every day, start a new page. Make a notation every single time you spend money, whether you use cash, credit, check, or debit. Note how much you spent and on what. Be precise.

Don't forget to write down payments that are subtracted from your bank accounts automatically.

Then, once or twice a week (twice is actually easier and therefore better, in my opinion), total up how much you have spent overall and in different categories.

This is where this habit becomes an incredibly useful tool for getting clear about your behavior and the meaning and value to you of your choices. This is a wonderful way to identify areas where you can reallocate resources. Once you have the figures for the week in front of you, you can make decisions about where to cut back if you're overspending.

In addition, most people discover that they have some categories where their spending is a bit out of control. Food, clothing, and books are common themes I see.

I usually recommend that my clients get really specific when it comes to food. Many of us eat when we're stressed. A friend of mine used to reward herself with expensive wine and cheese when she was on a deadline to complete a project. She felt that she deserved to be pampered. But she had no idea how much she was spending until I suggested she tally her receipts from the previous month. That's when she was shocked to discover that the amount was roughly equivalent to what she owed on her monthly credit card statements. I asked her, "Is the expense worth it to you?"

It's often a good idea to monitor your spending on stress-eating foods. For instance, I track my ice cream purchases separately. Some of my clients monitor their spending on chocolate. Others, who have a predilection for salty or crunchy treats, track spending on those.

Once a month, make an appointment with yourself to add up your weekly figures. The detailed data in certain areas can really shine the light on your spending blind spots!

One area that often goes unnoticed until people begin reviewing expenses from their bank statements is the area of recurring automatic payments. How many of these do you have? Do you even recognize them anymore? Are they really yours? (One of my clients discovered a fraudulent charge that had been recurring for almost a year before she noticed it.) Are you really using what you're paying for? Could you cancel the service now and save that money? If you find yourself hesitating about cancelling a subscription, multiply the monthly payment times twelve (what it costs for a year) and ask yourself if it's really necessary.

HABIT 10

SUPERVISE YOUR BOOKKEEPER'S DECISIONS

A common mistake coaches and holistic business owners make is leaving routine financial decisions to a bookkeeper.

Having a bookkeeping system is an important aspect of running a successful business. You may need to hire a bookkeeper to set one up for you, especially if you feel like you're not a "numbers" person. However, you can't assume that bookkeepers are perfect or that they'll always make the best decisions for your business.

Don't get me wrong, it's important to keep track of your numbers, and bookkeepers can go a long way toward making your accounting easier. The trouble comes when you rely on a bookkeeper to substitute his or her judgment for yours.

You need to realize that IT'S NOT THE BOOKKEEPER'S MONEY.

Your bookkeeper may not share the same priorities and values that you have with money. Your bookkeeper might not have great work habits.

Your bookkeeper's main focus may be to pay the bills with whatever money is in your account, which could empty your account too quickly. That kind of decision could end up hurting your business by constricting your cash flow.

Supervise your bookkeeper by staying in regular communication and balancing the accounts a minimum of once a month when the new bank statement comes in. Also set a policy that you have to approve every outgoing payment—even prescheduled ones.

───※───

You may want to hire a money coach to help you figure out your priorities, discover your emotional triggers and blind spots regarding spending and income, and train you in the practical skills of financial management.

───※───

HABIT 11

REGULARLY GIVE YOURSELF TIME OFF

"*How can I even think about taking time off if I am a one-woman (one-man) show? If I'm not working, I'm not making money.*"

Perhaps you've had this thought yourself if you've been in business for a while. It's another one of those secrets about having one's own coaching business where you get paid by the hour that doesn't get mentioned at the start. Instead, many coaches, wanting to put on a brave face for the world, will expound on the advantages of being able to work only when they want to.

As great as it is to be your own boss, the truth is that reality sets in when those who've started their own businesses discover that they work longer and harder as entrepreneurs than they ever did as employees in someone else's business.

It's very common that the boss—that's you—thinks you have to work constantly to keep the money flowing in. This is especially true if you're paid by the hour for your services.

The trouble is that when you push yourself to work nearly every day, week in and week out, you lose your sparkle.

Your work begins to feel like an obligation, rather than fun, and it's difficult to be creative. But what if there was another option? What would that look like for you? What would that do for you?

At the very least, it's important to give yourself permission (if you won't, who will?) to take at least one long weekend a month to step away from your business.

Years ago, a colleague of mine surprised me when she told me that she takes three whole months off from working with clients each year: April, August, and December. Of course, these months weren't all devoted to play. Some of that time was spent focusing on her creative work. But she literally took a break from her clients for a month at a time.

I don't know about you, but I think that is fabulous idea and a habit we should all emulate!

During the "down" months, you could completely unplug for a few weeks. It's also a great time for you to attend retreats and trainings and really be focused, since you're not worried about what's happening back in your business.

Wouldn't it be wonderful to fully participate and enjoy the holidays without trying to juggle business commitments?

Imagine how excited you would be to catch up with your clients after a month. They benefit as well from additional time to integrate their shifts/growth.

Imagine how great you'd feel if you treated yourself to even a half day off once a week to do something you enjoyed. Time to totally unplug from your phone and email. With my private clients, I show them how they can not only spend weeks away from their business, but also how to pay themselves while doing so.

HABIT 12

SHARE THE WEALTH WITH YOURSELF

Many times my clients ask me what to do with big chunks of income. As strange as it sounds, unusually large sums can really throw us off our money game.

We'll assume that your "windfall" is the result of promoting your new group program two or three times a year, or of having begun doing joint ventures. Maybe you finally added your high-end VIP program or started selling from the stage.

Your windfall might come from another source, of course, like the sale of property, an annual bonus, or the repayment of a loan. It could also be money from an inheritance.

For some reason, when we receive money that is outside of our normal schedule and/or amount, we tend to look at it differently than the money we earn with each client or paycheck. It seems less real or something. And it can wreak havoc on your financial stability if you're not careful.

That's why so many lottery winners end up broke and struggling.

When a windfall comes in, it's extremely important to approach spending decisions with a sense of moderation. Too often, people who receive a windfall abandon caution and end up spending more than comes in. Rather than helping them accomplish their financial goals, in such cases getting a windfall actually puts them in a worse position than beforehand.

One way to avoid this pitfall is to resist the urge to spend it mentally before it shows up in your bank account. Wait until you see the exact amount after taxes, and so forth, before you make your purchase decision.

What to Do with a Windfall

For a balanced approach, big chunks of money are best divided into three parts: Past, Present, and Future. The parts don't have to be equal amounts, as in thirds. Your split might look more like 25 percent (Past), 25 percent (Present), and 50 percent (Future).

If you have debt, you may choose 50 percent (Past), 25 percent (Present), and 25 percent (Future). Use the largest portion to pay down your debt. Another portion is for your Crystal Ball Fund.

The other portion goes into fulfilling your current needs, wants, and desires. Look at areas of your business where you may have been making do or doing without and where you might be dealing with daily irritations. Maybe it's time to spruce up your office or bring on team member. Perhaps you will finally delegate those parts of your business that you dislike doing (but still need to get done).

This is really interesting and juicy territory to explore. Because of this, I offer ongoing twenty-one-day group trainings on this. Learn more and sign up on my website: www.EmbracingMoney.com.

HABIT 13

KNOW HOW MUCH IS REALLY COMING IN

When you read about this habit, it may seem overly simple. For someone else, it might prompt a huge "aha" moment. Just know that any way it lands for you is perfect.

If you're currently experiencing a tight cash flow, it's easy to become so intently focused on the small chunks of money that come in each week and the next bills that must get paid from them that you begin feeling stuck in a pattern of "not enough" or "barely enough" thinking.

Perhaps you can't see the forest for the trees. The trees are the small chunks of money that come in. The forest is your monthly income, when all the chunks are added up.

But what would it do for you if you stepped back and looked at the forest, the TOTAL of all those tiny chunks of income on a monthly basis? And what about on annual basis? Get into the habit of doing so and I predict that you'll have a much different perspective—a higher vision—of your business. If you're already looking at your monthly totals, then your challenge (your forest) is to know your annual income.

Implementing this habit will help you make more grounded decisions about your business growth.

HABIT 14

BASE THIS MONTH'S SPENDING ON LAST MONTH'S INCOME

This strategy alone will keep you from going into debt or taking on more debt than you already have. It's especially important if your income fluctuates. Up and down income levels are a common experience for most business owners.

Take a moment to embrace the simplicity of the habit of basing this month's spending on last month's income.

If you paid attention to how much money came in last month, and you set a threshold for this month's spending in advance, then you can skillfully avoid taking on any debt this month.

With this habit, you get to choose consciously how much to spend and know that you are going to—at the very least—break even this month.

How Can You Implement This Habit?

If you've already implemented Habit 13, "Know How Much Is Really Coming In," then you're ready for this one.

A very simplified way to do this is to carry a small notebook or even an index card in your pocketbook. You are going to create a version of a checkbook register (the difference is that this one won't allow for new income).

Write down how much income you brought in last month in the upper right-hand corner of your notebook page. Each time you spend money, create an entry for it by writing down what you spent it on and how much you spent.

Subtract the amount of that entry from your income from last month.

This will leave you with a new remaining balance.
By doing the math each time you make expenditure, you'll always have a running tally that shows you how much money you can safely spend this month without taking on new debt.

As you watch the remainder of your allotment going down, pay close attention to your spending behavior. Your goal is to have a positive number left at the end of the month. This is what's meant by the term *financial stability:* consistently spending the same or less than you earned last month.

Wash, rinse, repeat!

Of course, there will be times when you have to spend more money than you brought in during the preceding month. That's just life. Some months expenses are higher than other months because of occasional expenses like the cost of car repairs, insurance premiums, tuition, and so on.

Review Habit 2 (see page 3) for help in saving ahead of time for occasional expenses.

If you want to fast-track this habit, you can figure out what your income last month was by reviewing your bank statement for deposits. Add up all the deposits (assuming they were all from income) and use that number to designate your baseline for this month's spending.

HABIT 15

ACHIEVE YOUR DREAMS BY CREATING A BUSINESS SPENDING PLAN

Before you get the idea that this is a budget—and potentially restrictive—it's not. It's about designing your life, first and foremost. And creating a financial structure that is tailored just for you.

It's this *structure* that brings TRUE financial freedom, which is the freedom to choose what you do with your money. Having this structure in place allows you to do and have more, not less.

Knowing exactly what's going on financially allows you to relax and stop stressing about money.

With my clients and in my own life, I use an online tool for this process. It is many times more powerful than using this paper method, but I wanted to give you a way to do this on your own so you could get started today.

In this habit, we are going to expand on the process of tracking your cash flow so you can actually predict how your month will end. By that I mean you can determine how much money you will have left at the end of the month, so you know you can easily pay any bills that are due early in the month, like rent or utilities.

Implementing this process will eliminate or at least reduce many sleepless nights caused by financial worries.

Here's How This Works

Start with a fresh calendar for the upcoming month. You'll probably want to use a different color ink for this part, so that you can clearly see this is your original plan.

At the top of the calendar, write down a prediction for how much money will be in your bank account at the end of the day on the last day of the month.

How do you formulate this number? It's easy: You'll add up three numbers.

If you're planning for June, ask yourself how much money you had in your account on May 31 at 11 pm. That's your first figure.

Your next two figures come from reviewing your anticipated income for the month.

Use the past few months' cash flow tracking as a guide to come up with the second figure.

Also take into consideration any new business you feel pretty certain will turn into real dollars this month. That's the third figure. Add this number to the other two numbers.

The resulting tally is the total amount available for this month (without taking on any debt).

Once you know your total anticipated income, you'll work on anticipating your total expenses for the month.

Using the data you collected about your expenses from the past couple of months, come up with a figure for your anticipated expenses.

Subtract your total anticipated expenses from the total anticipated income available for the month. The result of this equation is how much money you should have left at the end of the month after all of your spending.

As long as your projections are pretty accurate you'll now have clarity on your monthly finances. This will enable you to be a better planner. The goal is to have a remainder and not be at zero at the end of the month.

Remember, most businesses have bills that need to be paid on the first of each month, or soon after, so there needs to be money left in your account on the last day of the month to cover these and have a cushion.

A good target is to end one month (let's say June) with twice the dollar amount of expenses that are due during the first week of the next month (in this case, July). For even better cash flow, shoot for closer to three times that number.

When you use this simple process, you'll know in advance how much money will be left at the end of the month, before it even starts! This does wonders for your peace of mind.

An example:

Beginning of the month balance	$2,600
Add anticipated income	$4,200
Amount of money available to spend	$6,800
Subtract anticipated expenses	($3,300)
Your balance at the end of the month	$3,500

HABIT 16

RESIST THE URGE TO PAY OFF DEBT QUICKLY

While debt can be nerve-wracking and uncomfortable, if you want to be free of it, or at least in control of it, then read what I have to say about this habit at least three times. Then implement it!

The reason most debt pay-off strategies fail is that people focus all their energy and effort on their debt and none of their energy on creating financial stability.

Financial stability is what will get you out of debt and KEEP you out of debt. For good. Forever.

The first thing you want to do is create a foundation of stability in your finances. That means that you are:

- Consistently spending less than you bring in.
- Your debt is not growing.
- You're putting money into savings on a regular basis.

Once you've achieved financial stability, *then* start paying down your debt in a reasonable and sustainable fashion.

It's important to build your savings habit *first*, before paying down debt. Trying to pay off debt before achieving financial stability is the reason many people get stuck in a cycle of getting out of debt and then getting right back into it again.

The last thing you want to do is constrict your life to pay off your debt faster. Why? Because it's like being on a low-calorie diet. Sure, it feels good the first week to see the pounds come off. But soon you feel deprived and irritable. Eventually you will rebel and indulge in an eating—or spending—binge.

Come on. We've all done it. With either food or money—and probably with both. Right? I know I have.

Not only won't you feel deprived if you resist the urge to pay off debt too quickly, you'll feel proud of yourself and your ability to make smart and meaningful decisions.

HABIT 17

SEEK OUT SEXY SUBSTITUTIONS

Instead of constriction, we want *expansion*. How can you meet your needs today in creative ways that may cost a bit less so that you can still have an enjoyable life while you're paying a bit extra each month on your credit card debt?

It might mean checking out consignment shops for gently used clothes instead of paying full price. You might be surprised how many items still have the original price tags on them. (I recently found a fantastic linen suit that fit me well at a consignment shop for only $20!)

It might mean buying high-quality coffee and brewing it at home instead of buying it out.

It could be buying used books on Amazon or from a local used bookstore instead of buying brand-new ones. Better yet, be green and borrow books from the library.

Maybe for you a sexy substitution looks like planting container gardens and growing some vegetables yourself instead of paying for organic store-bought produce.

If you ask yourself, "What is the underlying need that I am trying to satisfy with this purchase/experience? How else might I meet this need?" and then listen to what shows up. Our minds are wired to answer questions. When you learn to ask the right questions, you will find new ways of meeting your needs for less or no cost. I promise.

HABIT 18

HIT THE PAUSE BUTTON

This habit may seem like a no-brainer, but I'm going to include it anyway.

Hold off on making money decisions when you're feeling emotional. It could be any emotion, really, but in particular I'm referring to being hungry, angry, lonely, and tired.

Habit 18 is to H.A.L.T.

I'm not talking just about purchases here; I'm referring to ALL financial transactions, including making investment decisions.

It may not even be a specific transaction; it may be another decision relating to your business.

When a colleague first shared this one with me, my thoughts immediately went to "retail therapy" (buying something to comfort yourself). However, after mulling it over, I realized that it could also occur as a decision to deny oneself.

A client once shared that in the year prior to working with me she had lost a dear relative who lived a plane ride away. She believed that she couldn't afford to go to the funeral, so she regretfully missed out on saying goodbye in the presence of other loved ones. After getting to know more about her money situation, I could see that she actually did have the financial resources to purchase a ticket and cover the other travel expenses. But she couldn't see that as an option, because she was in the habit of leading a restricted lifestyle.

Since money issues show up along a spectrum, this type of behavior is at the opposite end from the "retail therapy" behavior and thought processes.

In the case of an ongoing or long-term emotional situation, such as grief, it's even more important to postpone money decisions than it is normally.

When my father died in an accident when I was twenty-one years old, my mother was just fifty.

I remember one night she was really mad at my brother and me. For some reason she believed we wanted her money. (What we really wanted was for her to move forward and to allow us to do the same.) In the midst of her anger she wrote each of us a check for one-third of the insurance benefit she'd received. Of course we tore them up!

I believe it was her Uncle Lyle who wisely told her not to make any big decisions, financial or otherwise, for at least a year.

As a result of following that advice (and adding a few years just to be sure), my mother has been able to create financial stability that will last her for her entire life. And with our family's genes, that will likely take her into her late nineties!

HABIT 19

DOWNSIZE YOUR SPENDING WHILE YOUR BUSINESS RAMPS UP

I really want to emphasize this habit.
    Why? Because I've seen too many businesses (not my clients, thankfully) go under because the owners were using their business cash flow to support their personal lives. They were literally taking money out of their cash drawer and using it for dinner and drinks on the town, or paying for a luxury car, and calling it a business expense.

This is NOT the right way to support your business. For the first five years (at least), your business is going to be in a fragile state, even if it's growing significantly. *Especially* if it's growing significantly.

Fast growth is even more difficult to support than slow growth. All of the many parts of your business are moving faster. The revenue is up, yes, but the systems, staff, and other resources needed to support this increase are up as well, usually at a higher percentage than the revenue growth.

So while revenue is up, profits (by percentage) are usually down. Not knowing this can cause you to make decisions based on false information, which could throw a monkey wrench into your cash flow machine. Since cash flow is the key to any successful business, do yourself a favor and invest in a money coach. Learn to do things correctly early on and you'll avoid making costly mistakes.

Knowing there is an objective person on your side, guiding you to implement systems to support the health of your business and your financial life as a whole, will pay for itself many times over.

It will be the best investment you could ever make in your business. (That comes from my clients' feedback, not from me.)

HABIT 20

CONNECT WITH YOUR CREDIT CARDS

Credits cards can be useful—and they can be very confusing. The confusion comes from having the spending and amount due spread over two, and sometimes three, calendar months. It's very challenging to be in "real time" with your money, especially when you're paying this month for purchases made last month or the month before.

When this happens, it's hard to determine how much was spent in each month, and how much is owed for each month specifically.

An easy way to escape from this bit of financial fog is to move your due dates to the end of the month. For example, to the 29th or 30th.

It may seem like an insignificant thing, but this practice can make it much clearer to see what's really going on with your credit card spending and balances.

The following strategy is especially helpful if you're on a plan to stop adding to your existing balances.

You simply log in to your account just before your due date and see what your New Purchase total is. Pay that amount on your due date, along with an amount you've designated to pay down the outstanding balance (older debt).

By paying all new charges each month just before the due date, you effectively stop the financial bleeding—and halt the growth—of your credit card debt.

Tweak this habit to create even more discipline by paying off new purchases on a weekly basis. Simply add up all new charges for the past seven to ten days (to allow for pending charges) and make an online payment each week.

Because the weekly balance you pay off each week is a smaller amount than a monthly balance would be, it can be easier on your cash flow. Another benefit is that it makes you that much more conscious of your week-to-week spending.

HABIT 21

KEEP IT CLEAN WITH UNCLE SAM

Taxes can be a nightmare for a coach or holistic business owner, especially the first year or two when they usually are tempted to forego paying quarterly estimated taxes.

Business owners who don't plan in advance for their taxes often spend the rest of the year paying off what they owe to the IRS. They barely get through their payment plan, and then they need to start all over again the next tax year.

I hope this doesn't happen to you. It won't if you develop the habit of sweeping 20–25 percent of your income into a savings account specifically for your tax payments. The higher your revenue, the more you want to be putting aside.

Pretend this savings account is not there, not accessible, and you will be thrilled when your next tax payment comes due.

You could save your estimated tax liability in your Crystal Ball Account or create one specifically for taxes. If you plan for this in advance you'll save yourself a ton of stress every quarter and especially each April.

Let me step up on my soapbox again for a moment, and caution you about something I hear way too often from business owners.

As a business owner, you will enjoy many tax benefits that employees cannot take advantage of, which reduces tax liability.

However, just because something is a tax-deductible business expense doesn't make it free. It still needs to be paid for out of your cash flow. So be careful not to fall into the habit of justifying purchases because "It's a tax write-off."

Let go of the idea that you're going to get a refund like you may have when you were an employee. It's probably a pipe dream. The reason for your refund was because your employer was taking the taxes out so you couldn't spend them.

Now, as a business owner, it's up to you to be disciplined. With self-discipline comes true freedom.

When you are self-disciplined, you are in control of your business, your money, and your life. You aren't at the mercy of your bills, your vendors, your landlord, or your mortgage company. You are truly able to make financial choices based on your values and desires.

That is real financial freedom!

ACKNOWLEDGMENTS

I would like to express my gratitude to Stephanie Gunning for her support and encouragement in seeing this book through to completion. Not only is she an extremely talented editor and publishing consultant, she's a marketing genius who has a keen eye for design. She's also a dear friend. Without her continued coaxing, this book would still be trapped inside of me. Thank you Stephanie!

RESOURCES

Visit Nancy's website, www.EmbracingMoney.com, to learn about her work and events. At Embracing Money, Nancy and her team are all about supporting you in transforming your relationship with money. How you experience money is influenced by your unique beliefs, habits, and history.

Join Other Readers

Connect with other readers of this book on the Facebook group created just for you!

Online Events

Join Nancy (and the Embracing Money community) for free and low-price workshops online. For a full list of opportunities, direct links, and bonus material visit:
www.EmbracingMoney.com/resources.

Connect with Nancy via Social Networks

Facebook: https://www.facebook.com/EmbracingMoney
Twitter: https://twitter.com/embracingmoney
LinkedIn: https://www.linkedin.com/in/nancyrevans

Group Coaching

Work with Nancy and be part of a supportive group of others committed to shifting their beliefs and circumstances around money. New groups form quarterly. To be notified of the next group launch, subscribe to Nancy's newsletter at: www.EmbracingMoney.com

Private Coaching Intensives

Kick start a transformation of your money habits and mindsets with a private coaching intensive with Nancy. Done by phone or Skype, these three- to four-hour sessions are a great way to accelerate positive change, stabilize cash flow, and reduce your stress around money. To purchase a session, contact: **info@EmbracingMoney.com**

Speaking

Nancy enjoys speaking about money to groups of all sizes. She delivers valuable content on a range of topics in 30–90-minute presentations. To request her media kit and have her speak at your event, contact: info@EmbracingMoney.com

ABOUT THE AUTHOR

NANCY RAE EVANS, Founder of Embracing Money, has over twenty years of experience helping business owners improve their cash flow.

A self-proclaimed numbers geek, she herself struggled to stabilize fluctuating income when she first stepped into the entrepreneurial lifestyle. After years of frustration followed by research and diligent study to figure out the secrets of financial management on her own, she succeeded. She now shares the strategies she embraces. These keep her sane and financially stable in an ever-changing world.

Nancy is passionate about teaching sound money habits and practices to conscious business owners, coaches, and holistic practitioners so their business can thrive and their gifts transform the world.

www.EmbracingMoney.com

WANT TO WRITE A BOOK AND GET IT PUBLISHED?

Discover how to become a successful author. Request a FREE consultation about your project with experts on self-publishing at Lincoln Square Books.

www.LincolnSquareBooks.com/consultation

1 (646) 355-0585

We helped Nancy Rae Evans publish her book. Why not you?

Ask us about our professional editing, consulting, design, and project management services. We're waiting to hear from you.

Stephanie Gunning, Founding Partner
Peter Rubie, Founding Partner

www.ingramcontent.com/pod-product-compliance
Lightning Source LLC
Chambersburg PA
CBHW060422050426
42449CB00009B/2091